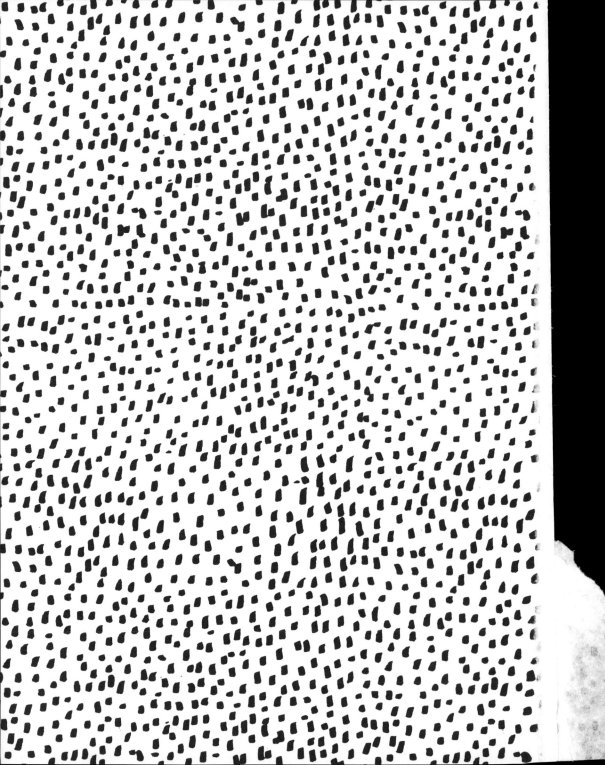

Words to Live By

52 weeks of possibility, one word at a time

Written & Compiled by Amelia Riedler

Designed by Emily Carlson

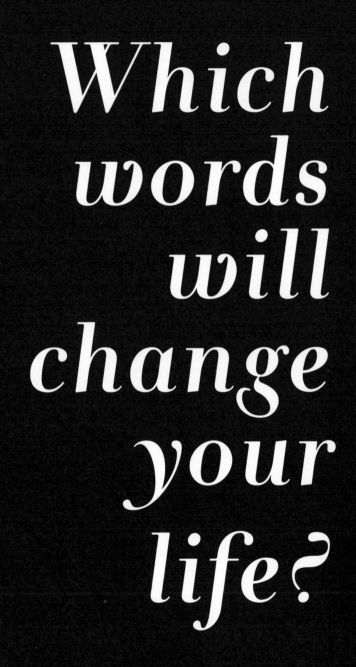

Which words will change your life?

The words in this journal are here to help you see your world differently. Simply pick a word for the week, live with it, be guided by it—and see where it takes you.

Each word has been chosen to help you see your life in new ways, from discovering what excites you to exploring what challenges you. From making room for more peace and growth to understanding what forgiveness can offer.

What will you see each week? What will you discover?

Start whenever and wherever you like. Move through the book in order or pick a word that feels right for that week. No matter how you complete this journal, just be sure to make space for these words in your life.

You'll soon see just how much possibility one year can hold.

ADV
ENT
URE

*Before me
lies the edge
of the world.
I am on my
way there
running.*

PAPAGO SONG

Adventure can be whatever you want it to be! An impromptu coffee or a trip to Paris. Is there something that excites you—big or small—that you could start planning this week?

Adventure

What about this personal adventure is so exciting to you?

Look

What we see depends mainly on what we look for.

SIR JOHN LUBBOCK

This week, use your powers of observation. Turn your attention outward. What do you see? Do you see the good? The bad? Everything in between? What haven't you noticed before?

In the middle of difficulty lies opportunity.

ALBERT EINSTEIN

Challenges can shape us and make us stronger. What's one challenge that excites you?

What challenges came to you this week? How did you overcome them?

...the very purpose of our life is to seek happiness.

DALAI LAMA

Choose your own word to focus on this week:

—————— *A few words to consider* ——————

STRENGTH · HEART · HAPPY

DETERMINED · TREASURE

Why did you pick the word you chose? What are you hoping it brings to you?

How did focusing on this word change things for you this week?

Create

Creativity is inventing, experimenting, growing, taking risks, breaking rules, making mistakes and having fun.

MARY LOU COOK

Creativity can be found in small things: the outfit you choose each day, the art you hang on your wall, even solving problems in a new way at work. In what ways are you regularly creative?

Are there any ways you'd like to add creativity to your life?

Take a moment to try one new activity this week.

SIM

PLE

Remember this, that very little is needed to make a happy life.

MARCUS AURELIUS

What does "simple" mean to you?

What things in your life are simple? Making a cup of tea, reading by lamplight, or perhaps working in a community garden. This week, notice all of the lovely, simple things you experience each day.

Every day do something that will inch you closer to a better tomorrow.

DOUG FIREBAUGH

Are there any things you're seeking to gain or change?
Either in your own personal growth or elsewhere in your life?

How often do you think about these changes? Each time you have these thoughts, you are in the process of seeking. Notice this week each time you find yourself seeking something bigger and better—and write it down here.

My will shall shape my future... only I hold the key to my destiny.

ELAINE MAXWELL

Choose your own word to focus on this week:

—— *A few words to consider* ——

VALUE · GIFTS · PASSION

RECOGNITION · FRIENDSHIP

Why did you pick the word you chose? What are you hoping it brings to you?

_____

_____

_____

_____

_____

_____

_____

_____

_____

How did focusing on this word change things for you this week?

_____

_____

_____

_____

_____

_____

_____

_____

Choosing words means choosing your intention.

Choosing the right words will guide you to the decisions you want to make—across all aspects of your life. Intentions don't have to be limited to one small single action, like "go to the gym more" or "increase my volunteer hours." Instead, if you shift these desires into a broader focus, such as "do things you're proud of" or "be fulfilled," you've provided yourself with a clear pathway for how you want to live your life. As business coach and writer Marla Tabaka notes, "Setting and living your intentions allows you to focus on who you are in the moment, to recognize and live your values, and to raise your emotional energy, which in turn raises your physical energy." In short, setting intentions has the power to change your life!

Happiness is not by chance, but by choice.

JIM ROHN

There are better things ahead than any we leave behind.

C. S. LEWIS

As the saying goes, the only constant thing in life is change. This week is about accepting change and seeing how much good can come of it. Where do you see change happening in your life right now?

Where would you like to see more change in your life?

Comfort

For happiness is anyone and anything at all that's loved by you.

CHARLES M. SCHULZ

Where do you find comfort? How do you feel in these moments?

_____

_____

_____

_____

_____

_____

_____

_____

_____

How do you like to give comfort to others? How do you like to receive comfort?

_____

_____

_____

_____

_____

_____

_____

_____

_____

Be afraid of nothing. You have within you all wisdom, all power, all strength, all understanding.

EILEEN CADDY

What makes a person powerful? In what ways are you already powerful?

Is there an area where you would like to reclaim your power? How could you start?

The secret of success is constancy to purpose.

BENJAMIN DISRAELI

Choose your own word to focus on this week:

```
┌─────────────────────────────────┐
│                                 │
│                                 │
│                                 │
└─────────────────────────────────┘
```

———— *A few words to consider* ————

IMPORTANT · KINDNESS · PREPARE

ENJOY · TENACITY

Why did you pick the word you chose? What are you hoping it brings to you?

How did focusing on this word change things for you this week?

Open

Greet each day with your eyes open to beauty, your mind open to change, and your heart open to love.

PAULA FINN

What does "being open" mean to you? In what ways are you open?

Take three instances this week, and they can be small, where your natural inclination was to defend, stop, or shy away. Use these experiences to shift your orientation. Notice why you had your initial reaction and record what it meant for you to "open up" in these moments.

Know the true value of time; snatch, seize, and enjoy every moment of it.

PHILIP DORMER STANHOPE

Every moment of the day can make a difference. Each "now" can bring a small change for the better or something big and wonderful that changes the course of the whole day. What times during this week were you most aware of moments like these? What did they reveal to you?

LOVE

...*everything in life responds to the song of the heart.*

ERNEST HOLMES

If you look with the right frame of mind, you can see love all around you. It doesn't even have to be love you're giving or receiving. You could overhear two coworkers enjoying each other's company, or someone could take the time to ask you a question. Where do you see love every day?

Your purpose is anything that touches your heart and makes a difference to you.

MARCIA WIEDER

Choose your own word to focus on this week:

———— *A few words to consider* ————

DRIVE · JOY · PRIDE

BRAVE · QUIET

Why did you pick the word you chose? What are you hoping it brings to you?

_____

_____

_____

_____

_____

_____

_____

_____

How did focusing on this word change things for you this week?

_____

_____

_____

_____

_____

_____

_____

_____

Follow the words.

Acclaimed author and motivational speaker Simon Sinek found his purpose by focusing on a single word. He had come to a point where he had lost his passion for his work in advertising; it had become a daily burden for him, and he found it took rather than restored his energy. He decided to focus on a single question: why? Through relentlessly asking himself this one word—in all aspects of his life—he discovered that his true passion was to

teach others, particularly leaders and businesses, how to inspire people. Fueled by this realization, Simon went on to share his philosophy with millions of others through books, talks, and seminars. Simon's story reminds us that when we communicate from the inside out—when we drive our own purpose rather than being driven by others—we can dramatically change how we're living our lives.

Step forward, each day, toward

what
you want.

Impact

Your spark can become a flame and change everything.

E. D. NIXON

Big acts aren't necessary to make a big impact. The right time, the right motivation, or consistent small acts can all make a difference. Look at each aspect of your life. Where can you see the impact you've made?

Patience

Patience is the companion of wisdom.

SAINT AUGUSTINE

Pay attention this week to at least three things that usually test your patience. If you can, simply let these moments happen— and see how you feel on the other end of them. Did trying to stay calm change anything for you?

INTUITION

Intuition

When your heart speaks, take good notes.

JUDITH EXNER

Have you ever had a feeling you should or shouldn't do something? These inklings can be easy to ignore, but they could be your intuition at work. This week, pay special attention. When did your intuition speak to you? What did it say?

To choose
is also
to begin.

STARHAWK

Choose your own word to focus on this week:

A few words to consider

IMAGINE · **BETTER** · **FAMILY**

SLOW · **FORWARD**

Why did you pick the word you chose? What are you hoping it brings to you?

_____

_____

_____

_____

_____

_____

_____

_____

_____

How did focusing on this word change things for you this week?

_____

_____

_____

_____

_____

_____

_____

_____

_____

*Close your
eyes and you
will see clearly.
Cease to listen
and you will
hear truth.
Be silent and
your heart
will sing.*

TAOIST MEDITATION

When do you feel free? Perhaps it's when you sip your morning coffee, or when you're laughing with friends. Perhaps it's when there is nothing you feel you "should" be doing. Note at least one moment each day when you feel free. If those moments aren't happening naturally, how can you add them to your day?

Want

Follow your desire as long as you live...

PTAHHOTEP

What are the things you yearn for, big and small? A decadent dessert? A chance to start your own business? Write down your wants here and then appreciate how these things tell you more about who you are.

All elements for your happiness are already here.

THICH NHAT HANH

Acceptance can offer relief, release, and even encouragement to move forward. It can be a step toward a place where you're more comfortable and happy. What are some things in your past you've had trouble accepting?

What are some things this week that would benefit from your acceptance?

We are created by the choices we make every day.

BERNIE SIEGEL

Choose your own word to focus on this week:

—— *A few words to consider* ——

LEAD · GIVE · RISK

LISTEN · EXAMINE

Why did you pick the word you chose? What are you hoping it brings to you?

_____

_____

_____

_____

_____

_____

_____

How did focusing on this word change things for you this week?

_____

_____

_____

_____

_____

_____

_____

_____

What words
are shaping
your future?

The way you think about words is the way you think about your life. Do you see words as just a practical tool? Or do you see the emotional power they can hold? Author, speaker, and philanthropist Tammy Kling tells us that "when [a word] comes into the mind [it] often settles in the heart." And once it's in your consciousness, it can be hard to get rid of—whether it's positive or negative.

She cautions us to move away from negative words because they can change how we see ourselves and even limit our possibilities. Meaning that negative words may create negative outcomes for us while positive words may open up positive ones. So think about who you are and what you want. Which words will you choose to tell your story?

Thoughts be things... cho good ones.

MIKE DOOLEY

come

ose the

With our thoughts and dreams we can bring anything into existence.

DIANE MARIECHILD

Every day is filled with ideas, whether you're deciding what to get at the grocery store or daydreaming about your next adventure. What ideas excite you the most?

This week, take time each day to brainstorm and appreciate all of the ideas you have. They can be wildly unrealistic ideas or completely practical. All can lead to something big, great, or good.

Surprise

Delight yourself in the surprises of today.

UNKNOWN

Do you like surprises? Why or why not? Perhaps you prefer certain kinds of surprises, such as receiving a gift or seeing a puppy walking down the street. What makes these kinds of surprises more enjoyable?

Find something every day that surprises you and note it here.

...the capacity to care is the thing which gives life its deepest significance.

PABLO CASALS

Responsibility can mean work, burden, and something to care for or worry about. But you often also take responsibility in areas that are important to you: your children, your work, your health. This week, try shifting your perspective to see how each of your responsibilities gives love to what you value. Where can you find joy and gratitude in the responsibilities you take?

...we make our lives by what we love.

JOHN CAGE

Choose your own word to focus on this week:

[   ]

———————— *A few words to consider* ————————

CONNECT · EXCITING · UNION

HARMONY · CALM

Why did you pick the word you chose? What are you hoping it brings to you?

How did focusing on this word change things for you this week?

With the new day comes new strength and new thoughts.

ELEANOR ROOSEVELT

Recall one negative past experience. It could be something big, such as an encounter that was challenging for you, or something smaller. Take some time to explore a few different explanations for what happened. Can you find some space to reconsider your experience?

Let your mind be quiet, realizing the beauty of the world, and the immense, the boundless treasures that it holds in store.

EDWARD CARPENTER

What does peace mean to you? How does this word make you feel?

When and where do you feel peace?

Choice

The key is to trust your heart...

AL SACHAROV

We make choices all day, every day—from the food we eat to the plans we make. Each choice creates a path, from where you're heading now to where you'll be heading in the future. Find some space this week to appreciate the sheer multitude of choices you make each day. List some of them here.

Choice

What choices in your past are you grateful you made? What choices were difficult for you?

...what we do today, right now, will have an accumulated effect on all our tomorrows.

ALEXANDRA STODDARD

Choose your own word to focus on this week:

A few words to consider

TRUST · PRIORITY · GRATITUDE

JOURNEY · PROGRESS

Why did you pick the word you chose? What are you hoping it brings to you?

How did focusing on this word change things for you this week?

Pick words to live your life by.

Shama Hyder—a well-known marketing guru—has tied everything she does in her life to a single quotation by Edward Teller: "When you get to the end of all the light you know, and it's time to step into the darkness of the unknown, faith is knowing that one of two things shall happen: either you will be given something solid to stand on, or you will be taught how to fly." With this quote as her guide, she started a prominent marketing company, and has been named a top entrepreneur by *Inc.*, *Business Week*, and *Forbes*. She's also been recognized by the White House and United Nations—among many other awards and honors. According to Shama, this quote embodies her belief that she should trust herself and the future—and always keep moving forward.

Is there a phrase or quotation that's always struck a chord with you? Write it down. Believe in it and see what happens.

_____

_____

Love your words.

Love
your
future.

Begin

It's time to start living the life you've imagined.

HENRY JAMES

What is one thing you'd like to begin this week? How will starting this thing make your life different?

WORTHY

I was always looking outside myself for strength and confidence, but it comes from within. It is there all the time.

ANNA FREUD

You may be assuming others don't think you're worthy, but sometimes it's only you who has doubt. Use this week to practice feeling that you are already worthy of the things you want. How did you tell yourself you were worthy in these moments?

Notice those moments where you hold back. Why do you think you hesitated to recognize your worth in these moments?

...new beauty meets us at every step in all our wanderings.

JOHN MUIR

Pay attention to new things that come your way this week.
What did you enjoy about these moments or experiences?

Setting a goal is like establishing a needle in your compass.

DAN ZADRA

Choose your own word to focus on this week:

―――――― *A few words to consider* ――――――

WILD · DELIGHT · LESS

SMILE · INTEGRITY

Why did you pick the word you chose? What are you hoping it brings to you?

How did focusing on this word change things for you this week?

Flow

Tension is who you think you should be. Relaxation is who you are.

CHINESE PROVERB

Our day is filled with plenty of transitions—between tasks, between places, between thoughts. Each of these moments, external or internal, is an opportunity to reduce our stress and to flow from one thing to the next. Focus on a few transitions you consistently encounter and record them here.

Do these transitions come easily to you? What are some things that would make them easier?

Fearless

Act as if it were impossible to fail.

DOROTHEA BRANDE

Being fearless takes practice. Start by doing one thing this week with a fearless state of mind. How did it feel?

Forgiveness is a virtue of the brave.

INDIRA GANDHI

Forgiveness can offer respite and release from anger or blame. This week isn't about actively forgiving—that can take a long time—but instead exploring what it might feel like if you did forgive. What is a situation where you would consider offering forgiveness?

What would you need for forgiveness to become a possibility?

No matter what anybody tells you, words and ideas can change the world.

DEAD POETS SOCIETY, 1989

Choose your own word to focus on this week:

— *A few words to consider* —

STILL · ENERGY · PLAN

FUNNY · PURE

Why did you pick the word you chose? What are you hoping it brings to you?

How did focusing on this word change things for you this week?

The
right
words
can
change
everything.

In the mid-1980s, Noah Levine was a young man facing a rough future. After years of violence and drug use, Noah was in prison and firmly on a path of self-destruction. But a single visit with his father—a Buddhist and Indian meditation teacher—changed his life. Noah's father asked him to focus on a single mission: "Focus all your attention on your breath. Count each inhalation and exhalation. Let go of the past and forget the future. Let your mind rest in the present."

That night in his cell, Noah chose to focus on these words and was immediately released from his typical thought patterns.

He dedicated himself to his personal mantra over the next several months, was eventually able to move to a halfway house, and then went on to earn a degree in counseling. With his education and his past in hand, Noah is now an author and has founded Against the Stream Buddhist Meditation Society, a drug and alcohol recovery program in LA, using his Buddhist teachings to help others.

What words can you focus on to help you stay grounded? What do you discover when you focus on the present?

...I am what I choose to become.

CARL JUNG

...be all alive,
body, soul,
mind, heart,
spirit.

THOMAS MERTON

MOVEMENT

Movement can be mental or physical, such as attending a dance class or thinking consciously about something that matters to you. Pay attention this week to all the ways you move, mentally and physically. What kinds of movement do you like the most? How do you feel afterward?

How else would you like to bring movement into your life?

...at the end of the day, your feet should be dirty, your hair messy and your eyes sparkling.

SHANTI

What excites you and entices you? Where do you find your joy?

What are some ways you'd like to add more enthusiasm to your days? List them here.

Conquer

Everything you want is on the other side of fear.

JACK CANFIELD

Look back, perhaps not even too far, and you'll find there are many things in your life that you've already conquered. These could be anything from baking a pie to developing healthy self-esteem. All took work and practice. What are some of the things you've conquered in your life?

What will you choose to conquer next? What steps can you take this week toward that goal?

You are only as strong as your purpose...

BARRY MUNRO

Choose your own word to focus on this week:

A few words to consider

ACTION · **SPIRIT** · **TODAY**

WARMTH · **ENDURANCE**

Why did you pick the word you chose? What are you hoping it brings to you?

How did focusing on this word change things for you this week?

Try

...you can, you should, and if you're brave enough to start, you will.

STEPHEN KING

What are two things you would like to try sometime in your life?

Are there any things you've regretted not trying? How could you try to recapture or start one of those experiences this week?

H E L P

...qualities of caring and responsiveness are the greatest gift we can offer.

TARTHANG TULKU

You may be surprised at how much others are willing to support you. Look for the ways that others help you this week. List some of them here.

Improvement

Every day is an opportunity to change things for the better.

MICHAEL PIVEC

Where do you want to see improvement in your life? Choose two areas to work on this week.

You may have a fresh start any moment you choose...

MARY PICKFORD

Choose your own word to focus on this week:

———————— A few words to consider ————————

WONDER · **OPPORTUNITY**

EMBRACE · **KEEP** · **GO**

Why did you pick the word you chose? What are you hoping it brings to you?

_____
_____
_____
_____
_____
_____
_____
_____

How did focusing on this word change things for you this week?

_____
_____
_____
_____
_____
_____
_____
_____

What words have the most meaning for you?

As noted in *Psychology Today*, "Words cannot change reality, but they can change how people perceive reality. Words create filters through which people view the world around them." Our brain is hardwired to hear words, to process language, and to understand meaning that can then create an emotional connection for us. Through our past, our everyday experiences, and our personality, certain words naturally come to have more meaning for us.

Are there any words and phrases that hold more meaning for you? Paying attention to these words is a wonderful insight into yourself—and it's a way to discover both your doubts and your desires.

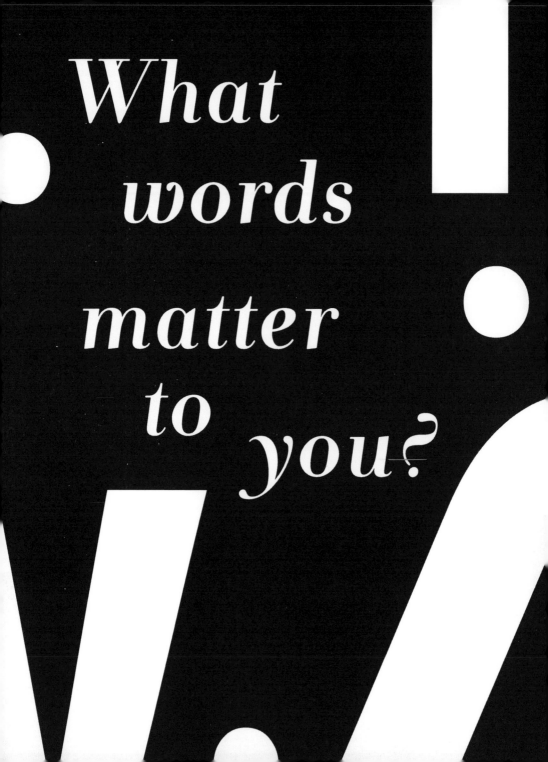

What words matter to you?

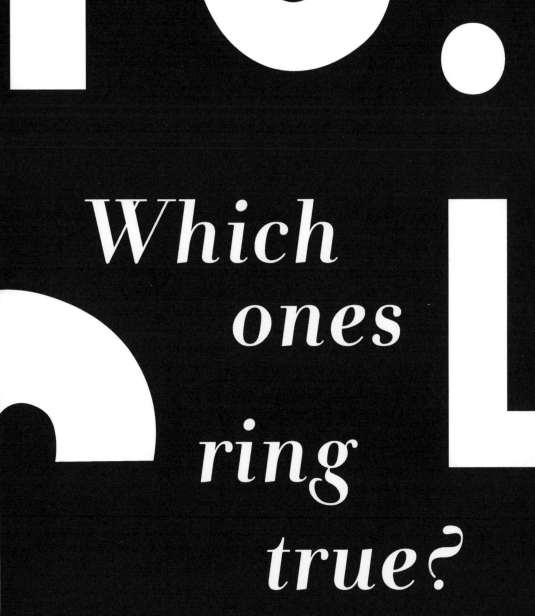

Which ones ring true?

Grow

Always be a work in progress.

UNKNOWN

There are many wonderful ways to grow. You can focus on your garden or your personal thoughts. You can grow a new business or perhaps help your children learn a new skill. Where would you like to grow this week?

Enjoy the journey, enjoy every moment...

MATT BIONDI

What kind of things do you like to explore? Places, feelings, or ideas? In what ways?

Choose a place, feeling, or idea you'd like to explore this week, and write down what your exploration revealed to you.

...memory is a way of holding on to the things you love, the things you are, the things you wish to never lose.

THE WONDER YEARS, 1988

What is one of your most significant memories? Who was there and how did you feel?

_____

_____

_____

_____

_____

_____

_____

_____

Record any moments this week that you want to remember. What made them important enough to write down?

_____

_____

_____

_____

_____

_____

_____

_____

This is where it all begins. Everything starts here, today.

DAVID NICHOLLS

Choose your own word to focus on this week:

—————— *A few words to consider* ——————

HOPE · DEEP · SILENCE

POSITIVE · TIME

Why did you pick the word you chose? What are you hoping it brings to you?

_____

_____

_____

_____

_____

_____

_____

_____

_____

How did focusing on this word change things for you this week?

_____

_____

_____

_____

_____

_____

_____

_____

_____

_____

My Favorite Words

Which words were most meaningful to you this year?

_____   _____

_____   _____

_____   _____

_____   _____

A Look Back

What possibilities came up this year? What new opportunities did you experience?

_____

_____

_____

_____

_____

_____

_____

_____

_____

_____

New Words to Explore

Write down a few words to focus on for the upcoming year and say why these words feel important to you.

A Look Forward

How do you feel about yourself, your life, and your world? What do you hope for most for the future?

Always remember that the future comes one day at a time.

DEAN ACHESON

With special thanks to the entire Compendium family.

Credits:

Written & Compiled by: Amelia Riedler
Designed by: Emily Carlson
Edited by: Ruth Austin

Library of Congress Control Number: 2018941326
ISBN: 978-1-946873-40-8

2nd printing. Printed in China with soy inks.